Contents

Introduction

The Earth is an amazing planet. It provides all the things that are needed for a huge variety of living things to flourish. Yet the Earth may now be under serious threat from one of the **species** for which it provides a home.

A major problem

Over the last 250 years, a booming human population has had a major impact on our planet. The development of large industries has made many, but not all countries and their people better off. Industries have provided jobs for many. Inventions and **technology** have improved the lives of millions of people. Yet many of the activities that have made this kind of growth possible are unsustainable. This means they cannot be continued in the same way forever. Humans are damaging their environment and using up parts of the natural world, such as tropical rainforests. There may not be any way to repair this damage.

❝Sustainable development is economic and social development that meets the needs of the current generation without undermining the ability of future generations to meet their own needs.❞

Our Common Future, The **Brundtland Commission**, 1987

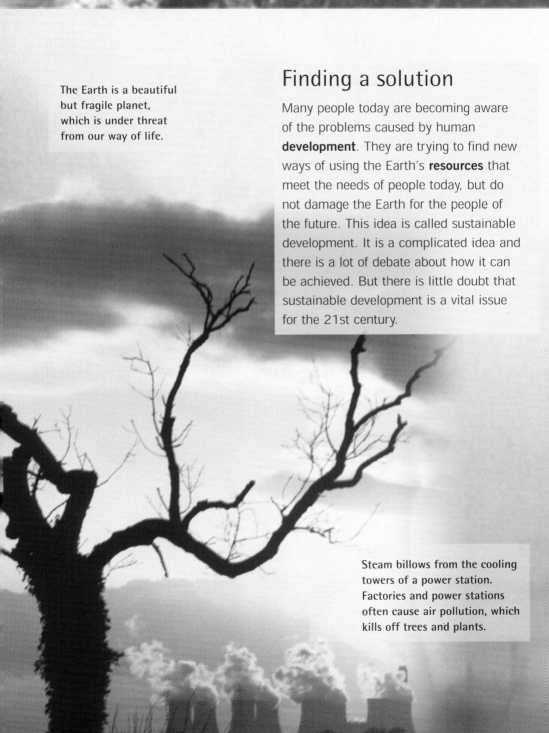

The Earth is a beautiful but fragile planet, which is under threat from our way of life.

Finding a solution

Many people today are becoming aware of the problems caused by human **development**. They are trying to find new ways of using the Earth's **resources** that meet the needs of people today, but do not damage the Earth for the people of the future. This idea is called sustainable development. It is a complicated idea and there is a lot of debate about how it can be achieved. But there is little doubt that sustainable development is a vital issue for the 21st century.

Steam billows from the cooling towers of a power station. Factories and power stations often cause air pollution, which kills off trees and plants.

What does sustainable development involve?

The process of human **development** involves finding ways to provide for people's needs. These needs are quite complex. People have **economic** needs – they need to be able to work in order to make money to live. But they also have **social** needs – such as healthcare and education. All of these needs have to be supplied by using **resources** provided by the Earth.

Some people believe that in order to save the planet, large parts of the Earth and its resources need to be left alone. They claim that the safety of the Earth must be placed before people's needs. However, people who support the idea of sustainable development suggest an alternative way of tackling the problem. They believe that it is acceptable to use some of the Earth's resources so long as they are used carefully. Using the Earth's resources in a **sustainable** way will mean that people in the future will also have the chance to use these resources.

Recycling materials is one way of preserving the Earth's resources for the future. Here, a pile of personal computers is being recycled.

Sustainable methods

People who believe in sustainable development aim to use **renewable resources** wherever possible. These are resources that can be replaced fairly easily, such as fast-growing forests or fast-breeding animals. They also try to use fewer **non-renewable resources**. These are resources, such as coal and oil, that once used up cannot be replaced. They aim to use all resources efficiently and fairly so that future generations will also be able to meet their needs.

As well as using resources carefully, people who believe in sustainable development aim to reduce pollution, such as air pollution or water pollution, which damages the ability of the Earth to support life. They also try not to damage the Earth, allowing its natural processes to continue and preserving homes for living things – both animals and plants.

An urgent issue

Many of these aims may sound like common sense. After all, who would want to use up all of something that cannot be replaced? And who would want to damage the Earth's ability to provide a home for billions of creatures? The answer is – human beings. Individuals, groups, companies and governments have all lived in ways that are not sustainable. The Earth has existed for over four billion years, yet most of the damage done to it has happened in the last 250 years. The rate of damage is speeding up very fast. This is why the issue of sustainable development has become so important in recent times.

Forests of fast-growing conifers are often known as 'sustainable forests' because new trees are constantly planted to replace the ones that are cut down.

❝Treat the Earth well. It is not inherited from your parents, it is borrowed from your children.❞

Old Kenyan proverb

Human impact

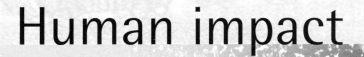

For thousands of years, people did not cause the planet any serious harm. Most very early people were nomadic – wandering from place to place in order to hunt and gather foods. Over time, as people learned to grow crops and raise animals, they stayed in one place and started to have more impact on the land and water around them. They began to clear small plots of land in order to plant crops or divert streams and rivers to water fields. But these first changes to the environment were very minor.

As the human population grew in number and advanced in knowledge, they began to have more impact on the Earth. Large areas of woodland were cut down to clear land for farming, and wood was also used to build houses and ships. Rocks which contained metals were mined from the Earth's surface and the first great cities started to grow.

During the 19th century, increased industrial activity caused huge amounts of pollution, which went completely unchecked.

The Industrial Revolution

In the late 18th century, the **Industrial Revolution** began in Europe and rapidly spread to the USA. For the first time, huge numbers of goods, such as clothing, could be produced cheaply and quickly in factories full of machinery. Demand soared for **raw materials**, such as cotton and wool, to make the goods. Metals were needed to make the new machinery, and machines needed fuels, such as coal and oil, to run. Large areas of the natural world were damaged in the rush to mine metals, extract fuels and gather or grow certain raw materials.

The rapid increase in the world's population has put a great strain on the Earth's resources. This photograph shows a crowded city street in China, where the population is growing at a rate of more than 11 million people per year.

Transport and pollution

The invention of motorized transport at the end of the 19th century changed the way that people moved around the planet. It also used up even more **resources**. Different methods of transport, and particularly cars, have added greatly to the problems of pollution caused by industry. This pollution not only damages the air, but also affects soil, water, plants and animals.

Population explosion

By the beginning of the 19th century, the world population was growing at an incredible rate. This was due to many changes, including advances in medicine and improved public hygiene, which helped to lower the number of very early deaths and also meant that people generally lived for longer.

In 1750, there were around 700 million people on Earth. By 1960, that number was over 3 billion. In 1999, the human population passed the 6 billion mark. The drive to provide for such large numbers of people has resulted in the Earth being plundered for food, fuel and raw materials.

Understanding the Earth

As the **Industrial Revolution** ploughed ahead in the 19th and 20th centuries, the damage done to the Earth was either not understood or not given a second thought. However, in the second half of the 20th century scientific research started to highlight the real problems caused by such rapid industrial **development**. For example, satellite images taken from space showed major **environmental** problems such as growing deserts. Studies of certain animals revealed that their numbers were dropping rapidly. People learned that more plant and animal **species** were at risk of dying out than had been previously thought.

Growing awareness

As new information about the state of the planet became available, a growing environmental or 'green' movement developed. Groups were formed such as the Sierra Club in the USA and Friends of the Earth in Europe. Members of these groups started to publicize issues such as air pollution and dangers to species, such as whales. Journalists also began to be aware of problems, such as the industrial pollution of the Great Lakes of the USA and Canada, and portrayed them in the media as environmental disasters. In 1967, the *Torrey Canyon* – one of the first giant oil supertankers – ran aground and over 31 million litres of oil leaked along the coasts of England and France, killing much sea life and over 25,000 birds. This dramatic accident helped to raise public awareness about the dangers of environmental pollution.

A clean-up team works to remove some of the thousands of litres of oil spilt by the Exxon Valdez oil tanker on the shores of Alaska in 1989. This was one of many oil spills, which have caused the death of millions of birds, fish and other wildlife.

"We are living on this planet as if we had another one to go to.**"**

Terri Swearingen, US Goldman Environmental Prize winner

The debate begins

By the 1970s, the damage to the environment was becoming hard to ignore. Important books and reports including *The Population Explosion* (by Paul R. Ehrlich) and *The Limits to Growth* (by Donella and Dennis Meadows, Jorgen Randers and William W. Behrens III) painted a gloomy picture of the future of the Earth. A growing number of people came to understand that the ways in which people were using the Earth could not be continued for ever.

Some people said development should be stopped and industries should be prevented from growing in order to save the environment. However, many others disagreed with such changes. Big businesses wanted to continue working in the way that had made them wealthy in the first place.

Many new or poor nations in Asia, Africa and South America wanted a chance to catch up with richer, more powerful nations so that they could look after their growing populations. These less developed nations argued that they had a right to use the same methods that had made other nations wealthy and powerful, even if these methods were unsustainable. With so many different viewpoints, there could be no simple solution.

First steps

In 1972, the **United Nations** held a Conference on the Human Environment. This was the first major meeting to concentrate world attention on **environmental** problems, and other conferences and reports soon followed. Most of the early meetings and reports focused on a single issue – either a major human problem, such as poverty, or a specific environmental problem, such as air pollution.

Gradually, more and more people started to see direct links between the different types of problems that affected the world. For example, the problem of the destruction of tropical rainforests in order to create more farmland is not just an environmental issue. It is also an **economic** problem because the people living in and near the rainforests may not have any alternatives to farming as ways to make their living.

The Brundtland Commission

In 1987, an important group with members from all over the world came together to discuss environmental problems and solutions. Those involved included politicians, their advisers, and experts in environmental issues and **social** development. The commission was headed by the first ever female prime minister of Norway, Gro Harlem Brundtland. In their report, called *Our Common Future*, the **Brundtland Commission** provided the most commonly used definition of sustainable development (see page 4).

The environmental pioneer Gro Harlem Brundtland visits a health centre in India. Brundtland was the head of the Brundtland Commission on sustainable development.

A balanced view

The Brundtland Commission members recognized strong links between the environment, the economy and people's lives together. They stated their belief that sustainable development could only work when environmental, economic and social needs were balanced. People do not just need a healthy Earth in order to live. They also need jobs, money, education, healthcare and communities. All of these things go together to create good living conditions, and all of these things need to be provided in ways that can be achieved both now and in the future.

The Earth Summit

The **Brundtland Commission** laid down some important principles for sustainable development. But the challenge remained of how these principles were to be put into practice.

The Rio Summit

Five years after the Brundtland Commission published its findings, the **United Nations (UN)** decided that it needed a progress report. It organized the United Nations Conference on Environment and Development (UNCED). This became known as the Earth **Summit**, or the Rio Summit because it was held in the city of Rio de Janeiro in Brazil. The Rio Summit was the biggest **environmental** conference the world had known. More than 30,000 people, including over 100 world leaders, attended the conference.

A number of important agreements were made at the Summit. The problems of **global warming** and the **enhanced greenhouse effect** (see page 23) were tackled by asking countries to cut the amount of **greenhouse gases** they sent into the **atmosphere**. An agreement called the Convention of Biological Diversity was set up to help preserve the world's plant and animal **species**. The longest of the five agreements was a 700-page document called **Agenda 21**, which was full of practical actions to create **sustainable** ways of living. These included plans for slowing down and stopping **deforestation** (the permanent destruction of forests) and for reducing rubbish, as well as suggestions for ways that local governments could involve local people in making decisions to improve their environment. Many schemes using Agenda 21 as a guideline have been put in place by countries including the UK, the USA and Australia.

Biological diversity

The term, biological diversity, (or **biodiversity**) is used to describe the range of different species of plants and animals found in a region or on the whole planet. The Earth is home to at least 14 million species. This incredible variety helps to support human life by providing a great range of foods, fuels, medicines and **raw materials**. Biodiversity also helps the planet provide natural services such clean air, drinkable water and fertile soils. Reducing biodiversity is unsustainable – species cannot be brought back from **extinction**. And with every species lost comes a greater chance that the Earth's natural services to its inhabitants cannot be performed as well as before.

The giant panda is one of many species threatened with extinction. Only around 1000 giant pandas survive in the wild.

The US Vice-President, Al Gore, with indigenous South Americans at the 1992 Earth Summit in Rio de Janeiro, Brazil.

15

Past mistakes

Supporters of sustainable development seek to find ways to care for and even improve the environment, while also looking after the **economy** and people's **social** needs. This is different to the way that **development** was seen in the past. Until recently, development tended to be thought of only in terms of the economy. Traditionally, a country's strength and performance has been measured by the value of the goods and services produced by that country. So development came to mean the increasing ability of a country to produce financial wealth through building up industries in order to turn more **resources** into goods and services. Continued growth of the economy was believed to be the way that people could progress and build better lives.

In the past, new and poorer countries were encouraged to follow the same path that had created countries with powerful economies such as the USA, Japan and the nations of Western Europe. The belief was that economic growth was the best or only way to fight human problems such as poverty and hunger.

The wrong approach?

During the 1960s and 1970s, some people began to question the traditional view of development. Many felt that the countries with the biggest and most developed economies didn't necessarily offer the most to their people. In many countries, economic growth had not improved the lives of most people – it had only benefited a small number of wealthy people. How money from the economy was used, who it went to and what services it was spent on became important questions.

A key idea in sustainable development is that development cannot be measured by economic statistics alone. Development is not just about money. It is also about the opportunities and freedoms in people's lives. Some experts began to measure a country's development in new ways. They did not simply look at what a country earned by its exports. Instead, they also studied a country's health and education statistics, such as how many people had access to clean water or the numbers of children in schools.

Supporters of sustainable development argue that economic success is not enough. In many parts of the world, thriving cities, such as Rio de Janeiro (shown here), are surrounded by slums. The challenge is to give all the people in a country a decent quality of life.

An unfair world

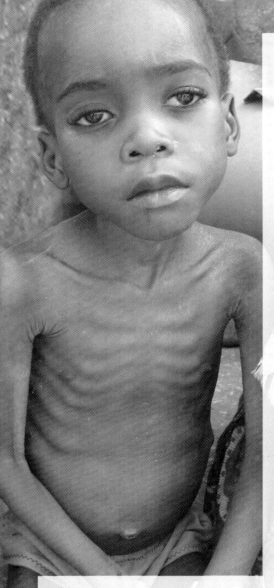

This boy from the African country of Angola suffers from malnutrition – caused by a severe lack of food. The United Nations World Food Programme estimates that there are more than 38 million victims of malnutrition in Africa alone.

The development gap

The **development** gap is one of the biggest problems faced by supporters of sustainable development. In the more developed nations, many people live comfortable lives which use up a large amount of the world's **resources** – for example, just 20 per cent of the world's population use 65 per cent of the world's energy supply. At the same time, millions of people in less developed countries have few opportunities to improve their lives and face extreme poverty, disease and early death. The average age of death of a person born in Angola, Rwanda or Zimbabwe, for example, is under 40, while someone born in Australia can expect to live to almost 80.

The rich countries are using up an unfair amount of the world's resources, while the poor countries face so many problems that their people have no time to think about the future or to find the best ways to achieve sustainable development. They are purely concerned with survival. For sustainable development to work, ways need to be found to close the development gap and put an end to the extreme poverty and hardship faced by hundreds of millions. Sustainable development cannot be achieved while there is such a great imbalance between the rich and poor nations of the world.

In 1950, the total output of the world **economy** was estimated to be 6.2 trillion (thousand billion) US dollars. In 2000, it had soared to 42 trillion. Whilst some people see this as proof of development's success, others point out that this growth has come at the cost of much **environmental** destruction and human misery. Development has definitely not resulted in equal benefits to people all over the planet. The vast difference in living conditions between most people in the more developed nations and many in the less developed nations is called the development gap.

More or less developed

The richer, industrial countries are found mainly in Europe, North America, Australasia and east Asia. The poorer nations tend to be found in Africa and South America and south Asia. In the past the rich nations were called developed and the poorer nations undeveloped or developing. In truth, all countries have some degree of development and even the richest are still developing. This is why 'more developed' and 'less developed' are the terms that are used today.

A boy from a wealthy, more developed nation plays in his bedroom surrounded by dozens of toys and games.

❝A global human society, characterized by islands of wealth, surrounded by a sea of poverty, is unsustainable.❞

Speech by Thabo Mbeki, President of South Africa, at the World Summit on Sustainable Development, Johannesburg, August 2002

Waste and water

Supporters of sustainable development call for people to produce and consume goods and services in ways which are fair and can be continued by future generations. This idea involves cutting back on the high levels of waste that people create. In Australia, for example, over 14 million tonnes of waste is deposited in giant holes, called landfill sites, every year. Further waste is burned, sometimes releasing harmful gases into the **atmosphere**, or is pumped into the sea. The USA is the major offender in this area. With less than 5 per cent of the world's population, it creates 50 per cent of the world's solid waste. Waste can be a pollutant, damaging the environment and spreading disease if it is not treated carefully. Waste also uses up valuable **resources**, such as land and energy, which are needed for its disposal.

Wasting water

The Earth's resources are either renewable – which means they can be created again – or non-renewable – which means that once they are used up they cannot be made again. Water is a **renewable resource**, but it can be both wasted and degraded – damaged so that it can no longer perform its function.

The polluting of rivers and lakes does not prevent them from existing, but it can stop them being able to support life or supply clean drinking water. People in more developed countries tend to take water for granted and waste it without thinking. But for many millions of people elsewhere, water is a life and death issue. Droughts and lack of water cause tens of thousands of deaths every year. Disease caused by dirty, polluted water is a far bigger killer, taking 4 million lives a year, according to the World Health Organization. The amount of clean water available for each person on the planet is declining fast.

> **Many of the wars of this century were about oil, but wars of the next century will be about water.**
>
> Ishmail Seageldin, Vice President of the World Bank, 1995

Water is a very precious resource. Here, a woman in Madagascar collects water from the only source in her village – a polluted pool.

Power and pollution

Industry depends on energy to provide power for its machines. Traditionally, the main fuels used as sources of energy have been natural gas, coal and oil. They are burned to create the power to drive engines or generate electricity.

Natural gas, coal and oil are all fossil fuels, which are **non-renewable resources**. Fossil fuels are made by squeezing together dead animal and plant matter within the Earth's crust over millions of years. Once they are used up, they cannot be renewed.

Fuel pollution problems

Scientists have shown that burning fossil fuels leads to a build up of gases in the **atmosphere**, which results in the **enhanced greenhouse effect** (see page 23). The consequence of this effect is **global warming**. If the enhanced greenhouse effect is not slowed down, there could be significant climate changes in the future, with widespread flooding, which would drive people out of their homes and cause many plants and animals to die out.

Pollution from burning fossil fuels affects our planet in other ways too. Some polluting substances in the atmosphere mix with the water vapour in clouds and fall as **acid rain**. Acid rain destroys trees and can stop lakes and rivers supporting life.

Alternative energy?

There are **sustainable** alternatives to the burning of fossil fuels, but most of them come with their own drawbacks. Wind power and **solar power** (power from the Sun) are two alternatives, but some areas of the world do not receive enough wind or direct sunlight to generate electricity continuously using **wind turbines** or **solar panels**.

Some sustainable energy sources can create **environmental** problems of their own. One example is hydroelectric power, which is used in many countries including the USA, Brazil and Canada. This form of power uses the energy in flowing water to generate electricity. But some larger hydroelectric schemes can have a massive effect on the local environment, involving damming rivers and creating artificial lakes that flood the land, displacing local people and destroying the **habitats** of animals and plants.

These trees have been destroyed by acid rain. Acid rain is caused by pollution in the atmosphere.

Enhanced greenhouse effect

Gases such as carbon dioxide and methane are found naturally in the Earth's atmosphere and are known as **greenhouse gases**. They perform an important job, trapping some of the Sun's energy as heat and helping to warm the planet's surface. This is called the greenhouse effect. But since the **Industrial Revolution**, levels of these gases in the atmosphere have risen by as much as 30 per cent. This has led to a problem, known as the enhanced greenhouse effect, when more heat is trapped and global temperatures rise. The main causes of the enhanced greenhouse effect are believed to be the burning of fossil fuels in factories and in motor vehicles, and the removal of much of the world's forest cover (see page 25).

The Glen Canyon dam and hydroelectric power plant, on the border of Arizona and Utah, USA, generates large amounts of electricity, but it also has a massive impact on the surrounding landscape.

The demands made by an increasing human population are placing **renewable resources**, such as forests and farmland, under threat. Forests are disappearing rapidly and deserts are growing at a rate of up to 60,000 square kilometres every year. Some of these changes are caused by natural alterations in climate but most are the result of human actions.

This farmer in the Amazon Basin of Brazil has slashed and burnt an area of rainforest to provide land for growing crops.

Losing farmland

The roots of trees and other plants help to hold the soil together and allow water to be absorbed into the soil. Removing plants through over-farming, clearing land or over-grazing livestock can all result in **soil erosion**. This occurs when good growing soil is washed or blown away because it has nothing to hold it in place. Water cannot easily be retained in this shifting soil and this can result in the development of desert-like regions in areas that were once important farmland.

Losing forests

Deforestation is the large-scale cutting down of trees. This is done to collect timber or to clear land for farming, mining or new towns. In the past 40 years, over 40 per cent of the world's forests have disappeared. This rate is obviously not **sustainable**. Forests are often described as the 'lungs of the planet' because they take in carbon dioxide from the **atmosphere** and send out oxygen – the gas which animals and humans need to survive. With fewer forests on the Earth, the vital job of exchanging carbon dioxide for oxygen cannot be done as well as before.

Vanishing rainforests

Rainforests exist in warm areas of the planet with heavy rainfall. The world's largest area of rainforest is in the Amazon Basin in South America but rainforests also exist in Africa, Asia and Australasia. Rainforests once covered 14 per cent of the Earth's land surface, but now they only cover 6 per cent. If the current rate of destruction is continued, there will be no rainforests at all in a hundred years' time.

Rainforests are the world's most **biodiverse** environments, providing homes for millions of different plants and animals. Many of the foods and medicines we use today first came from rainforests. Yet only 2 per cent of all the rainforest **species** have been tested by scientists. There could be many more cures for diseases still to be found, which people are now in danger of losing.

Can the Earth recover?

In the late 20th century, a number of people predicted that if our methods of **development** did not change, the human race was doomed. Some predicted that clean water, coal and oil would run out as early as 2000. Clearly, this hasn't happened. **Economic** development has continued, yet there is still clean water, coal and oil available on the Earth and humans still exist. Many people who think that sustainable development is unnecessary argue that the predictions being made today are also too gloomy. They believe that people underestimate the power of the Earth to renew itself and survive.

Others do not believe that the Earth has the power to look after itself, and maintain the capacity to support the increasing numbers of people living on it. They point to the facts that the amount of clean water is decreasing and the forests are disappearing. They also point out that the number of people on the Earth is increasing by 90 million or so every year. They fear that the Earth and its people will suffer terribly unless changes are made in the way that people live.

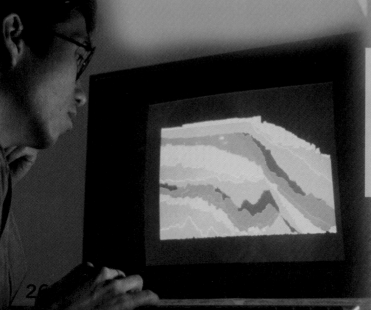

Some people believe that scientists will be able to discover all the resources we need for the future. Here, a technician examines a computer analysis of an area of land to see if it contains deposits of oil.

New solutions?

Another group believes that **environmental** groups underestimate people's ability to solve problems. The speed of **technology** has advanced rapidly. For example, 30 years ago, there were almost no personal computers and 20 years ago, the Internet did not exist. Who is to say that in the next 20 years, people will not be able to use technology to help them discover more resources, grow more food and solve the Earth's environmental problems?

However, many people disagree with this viewpoint. They think that sitting back and waiting for science and technology to solve our problems is a dangerous gamble. Our knowledge of how the Earth works is far from complete, and although human technology has advanced, it may never be capable of controlling events like droughts and earthquakes.

A helicopter sprays chemical pesticides on to a rice crop. Pesticides can build up in the soil and in rivers and lakes, damaging the Earth's precious resources.

Is it our problem?

The standard of living in countries like the USA, the UK and Australia has risen greatly in the past 40 years. Yet even the wealthiest countries have many issues to deal with, such as crime and the problem of homelessness. Surveys show that the majority of adults in wealthy countries want their own country's problems to be tackled before they look abroad. A number of people also think that the serious problems faced by another country are entirely that country's concern.

Many people oppose this view and feel that we live in a global community where problems are shared between nations. People who take this view believe that responsibilities cut across national boundaries. They believe that people must think more internationally if there are ever to be solutions. Many **environmental** problems, for instance, do not recognize national borders. **Acid rain** can be caused by industry in one country but fall on the lands of another, whilst **global warming** has the potential to affect everyone on the planet.

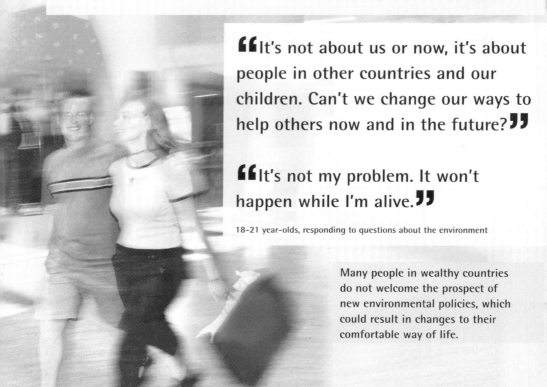

"It's not about us or now, it's about people in other countries and our children. Can't we change our ways to help others now and in the future?"

"It's not my problem. It won't happen while I'm alive."

18–21 year-olds, responding to questions about the environment

Many people in wealthy countries do not welcome the prospect of new environmental policies, which could result in changes to their comfortable way of life.

Today, not tomorrow?

Some people believe that any disasters which lie ahead are problems for people in the future to solve. Previous generations rarely planned ahead for us, so why should we plan for others? Critics of this view argue that previous generations did not choose **sustainable** ways of developing and this is a major reason why there are so many problems today. But we now know much more than before about how the Earth is being damaged. With greater understanding of our planet, why should we ignore the knowledge that we have gained or repeat the mistakes of the past?

A group of young demonstrators protest about the ways that development is affecting the planet. Some people believe passionately that these problems need to be solved as soon as possible.

Choosing to change

Changes to the ways individuals, societies, businesses and governments do things do not come easily. They can create extra costs, inconvenience and anger or upset. For example, a law that stops industries developing in a countryside area may be good for the environment, but it may clash with **economic** and **social** goals, by keeping people poor and out of work. So how do people decide which is the best way forward?

Making changes to the way we use **resources** involves many choices. Wind farms are an alternative method of producing energy, but people have mixed reactions to them. Some people object to the way they change the landscape, while others find them attractive.

How to choose?

One of the key problems in making a decision is finding ways to measure and compare different goals and targets. Some things, such as population size, can be quantified (given a value in numbers). Other things, such as the level of **environmental** damage in a region, are not so easy to measure. Some people think that there are just too many factors to consider, and so they decide that sustainable development may be unworkable. But other people try to meet the challenge of finding new ways of measuring and giving values to social and environmental factors.

Experts have developed a series of figures and measures called sustainable development indicators. These include figures about the economy, but also figures about the well-being of the population. For example, figures such as the number of people for every doctor, the number of children who die within their first year of life and the average age that people live to are used to help quantify and measure the health of a country's people. Other indicators measure the condition of parts of the environment. These include the level and type of air pollution, the amount of land that is turning into desert and the extent of forest areas that have been lost or damaged. Many people believe that when such figures are taken together they give a more accurate and rounded picture of the condition of a country than simple economic figures. They also make it easier to measure the levels of progress made in different areas and to compare different countries with one another.

Who decides?

The debate about who has the right to make decisions about sustainable development is a major one. **Agenda 21** – the practical agreement on sustainable development reached in 1992 – calls for as many people and groups as possible to be involved in making decisions. This, it states, is the only fair way for decisions to be made. However, some people feel that this can create major problems within a local or national government. Too many voices and opinions may lead to no decisions being taken.

On an international scale, the problem of who makes the decisions gets bigger and more complicated. Many people believe that the **United Nations** is the ideal place for discussion and decisions. Others feel that the UN is dominated by the more powerful nations, such as the USA, Japan and Germany, which tend to be more developed and have more economic wealth. Some less developed nations fear that they might be forced to agree to decisions made by more developed countries, who have been the biggest offenders in the past.

Pollution from a paper mill in the USA rises into the atmosphere. The USA is the world's most powerful nation but its record on pollution is not good.

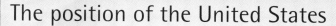

The position of the United States

Since the break-up of the **Soviet Union**, the United States has no rival for the role of the world's most powerful nation. Many people consider that this is good reason for the USA to take a major role in making decisions about the future of the Earth. However, others feel that the USA has been responsible for much of the world's unsustainable activity.

According to the US **environmental** group, The Sierra Club, in the 90 years from 1900 to 1990, the USA's population tripled, but its use of **raw materials** multiplied seventeen times. The United States today has less than 5 per cent of the world's population but uses a quarter of the world's oil and one third of the world's paper. Some people therefore wonder whether the USA, with its record, should be pressuring other, less developed nations to change.

The United States is the world's wealthiest and most powerful nation, but it has not been one of the leaders in sustainability. What sort of message does that send to poorer countries seeking ways to develop? Instead of listening to warnings from the USA and other more developed nations, it seems likely that less developed countries will be tempted to act in a similar way to the more developed nations.

Worldwide agreement

In less than 30 years, sustainable development has gone from being a new theory, to becoming the way that many people feel we should act in the future. Although progress has been slow in practical areas, there have also been a number of successes. Many of these successes are found at a local level, as communities **conserve** their **resources**, **recycle** more waste and try to live and work in more **sustainable** ways.

International successes

Some success has also been achieved at an international level. The governments of countries are meeting more and more often to discuss sustainable development issues. As well as holding discussions, countries have agreed on practical actions in some areas. For example, two **summits** held in 1987 and 1996 have led to treaties cutting back on the use of **CFCs** – chemicals which damage the **ozone layer** in the **atmosphere**. In 1986, 1.1 million tonnes of CFCs were used. Twelve years later, the figure was down to 156,000 tonnes and it is still falling, while the damage to the ozone layer appears to be slowing down.

The President of South Africa, Thabo Mbeki, at the opening of the 2002 World Summit on Sustainable Development, held in Johannesburg.

One of the aims of the Johannesburg Summit was to halve the number of people in the world without clean drinking water. Here, children in Nepal enjoy a drink at a water tap built by the charity WaterAid.

Johannesburg 2002

Ten years on from the Earth Summit at Rio de Janeiro, world leaders and thousands of scientists, experts and advisers met again, this time in Johannesburg, South Africa. There were criticisms of the scale of the event, which involved thousands of people, but many believe that the only way that agreements can be made is by holding large meetings in which all nations are involved.

Was Johannesburg 2002 a success or a failure? There is no simple answer. On the plus side, many new **initiatives** were announced. For example, governments agreed to a target of halving the number of people without clean drinking water and basic sanitation by 2015. On the minus side, some important issues were left undecided. For example, the Summit failed to agree on actual targets for the amount of energy that the world should produce by using sustainable sources such as wind and **solar power**.

ᏞᏞOur biggest challenge in this new century is to take an idea that seems abstract — sustainable development — and turn it into a reality for all the world's people.ᏜᏜ

Kofi Annan, UN Secretary General, describing the challenges of the 21st century at the Johannesburg Summit in 2002

Turning ideas into action

Turning agreements on sustainable development into action can take many years, and the benefits may only be seen tens of years ahead. Businesses, which are judged on their yearly profits, and governments, that are elected every few years, tend to concentrate on short-term projects that show benefits quickly. Choosing ways of acting which will only show benefits many years ahead can prove difficult for many organizations.

Government action

Despite these problems, many governments have found ways of promoting sustainable development. For example, the governments of many less developed nations are encouraging lower population growth. They are achieving this through increased awareness and education, especially by getting more girls into schools, and though more widespread use of family planning methods. Some governments also offer financial subsidies or penalties, rewarding smaller families and penalizing larger ones. The governments of some more developed nations are investing large sums of money into **sustainable** projects in other countries as well as funding research into sustainable forms of **technology** and energy. Some governments have created laws forcing companies that cause pollution to pay for the cost of their damage to the environment.

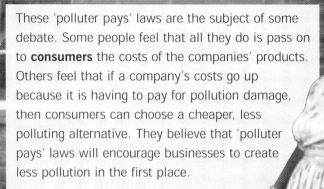

These 'polluter pays' laws are the subject of some debate. Some people feel that all they do is pass on to **consumers** the costs of the companies' products. Others feel that if a company's costs go up because it is having to pay for pollution damage, then consumers can choose a cheaper, less polluting alternative. They believe that 'polluter pays' laws will encourage businesses to create less pollution in the first place.

'Think global act local'

One of the most encouraging signs of progress towards sustainable development has taken place at a more local level. Over 6000 towns and cities all over the world have created their own local **Agenda 21** plan with targets to improve people's lives and the condition of their local environment in practical ways.

The African city of Dar es Salaam in Tanzania, for example, has improved the way it collects and gets rid of waste. Its scheme, which involves local people, has helped to cut back disease. Another project has been introduced in Holdfast Bay in South Australia. Here, local people have replanted native plants and installed barriers to protect their local sand-dune environment. These are just two of thousands of actions performed by local governments working with local people.

These girls are taking part in an outdoor class in Malawi, East Africa. Education is vital in order to give people a chance to improve their lives.

Sustainable energy

Conserving energy plays an important part in reducing unsustainable demands on the planet. Schemes which encourage people to waste less energy now exist in many nations. They take different forms, from publicizing ways to save electricity to paying part of the cost for businesses and individuals to switch to more energy-efficient devices. Many schemes have achieved a degree of success. For example, by using new EnergySaver lighting systems in its public places, the city of Chicago has cut its lighting energy use by a quarter in two years.

Renewable energy

Despite energy-saving schemes like the one in Chicago, world energy use is still rising. Many people believe that the key to **sustainable** energy is to switch to renewable energy sources such as the wind, sun, waves and tides. All of these sources can be harnessed to generate electricity. They create no air pollution and will not decrease in size over time.

People are making increasing use of renewable energy sources. For example, the number of **wind turbines** (electricity-generating windmills) has doubled in the past eight years. Denmark generates 10 per cent of its electricity in this way and plans for that figure to rise to 50 per cent by 2030. **Solar panels** now provide electricity in many places from the Olympic Stadium in Sydney, Australia, to schools in Africa and homes in California and Arizona, in the USA.

Lower cost energy

The sustainable energy issue is not just about how energy is generated or conserved. It is also about how energy can be applied to help encourage sustainable development in other areas. For example, whereas coal-fired and nuclear power stations cost hundreds of millions of dollars to build and run, small electricity generators using wind turbines and solar panels can be built on a far smaller scale and at much lower costs.

Wind and solar energy sources can be used to bring electricity to people in isolated areas. A recent **initiative** in Kenya, for instance, supplied a series of solar-powered fridges to store vaccines. This enabled many people to be immunized against diseases in out-of-the-way areas. New solar-powered lighting also allowed isolated Kenyan health centres to open at night and treat far more patients as a result.

These villagers in eastern Uganda are heating their food on a solar cooker. Solar cookers need only the heat of the sun for fuel, do not cause smoke pollution and save vital forest areas.

Sustainable food production

Experts believe that it is possible to feed the world in ways that do not damage the Earth beyond repair. Research has shown that there are many **sustainable** ways to grow crops, fish waters and rear livestock.

Sustainable farming

In many parts of the world, people are facing problems because their soil is losing its ability to support crops. This happens when the soil has had too many of its **nutrients** removed, has been polluted, or is being swept away by wind or water. One way of overcoming this problem is to sow a different crop in each growing season so that some crops put back nutrients into the soil that others take out. Other methods include using fewer chemicals in the growing process and planting trees and other natural barriers to avoid **soil erosion**. However, changes like these can result in added costs and smaller harvests. Sustainable farming isn't just an **environmental** issue – it is also about treating farmers and workers fairly.

Farmers in less developed nations often struggle to produce enough crops to make a living, especially in bad growing years. The world price of many basic crops rises and falls sharply and this can be devastating to small farms in less developed countries. Certain organizations, such as the European Fair Trade Association and the UK organization, The Fairtrade Foundation, now work with such farms. They offer farmers a constant, fair price for their crops, help small farms invest in sustainable farming methods and promote these crops to **consumers**. In 2001, over 44 million pounds worth of Fairtrade products were sold in UK stores.

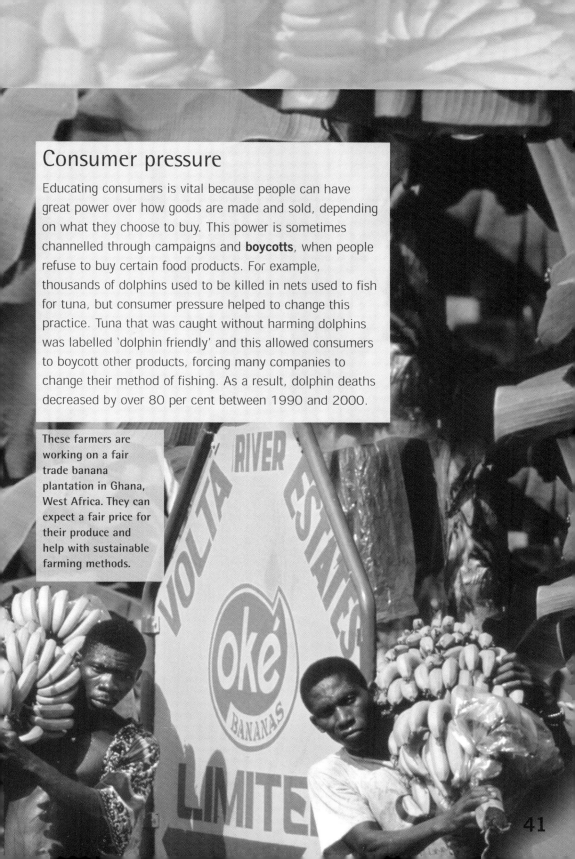

Consumer pressure

Educating consumers is vital because people can have great power over how goods are made and sold, depending on what they choose to buy. This power is sometimes channelled through campaigns and **boycotts**, when people refuse to buy certain food products. For example, thousands of dolphins used to be killed in nets used to fish for tuna, but consumer pressure helped to change this practice. Tuna that was caught without harming dolphins was labelled 'dolphin friendly' and this allowed consumers to boycott other products, forcing many companies to change their method of fishing. As a result, dolphin deaths decreased by over 80 per cent between 1990 and 2000.

These farmers are working on a fair trade banana plantation in Ghana, West Africa. They can expect a fair price for their produce and help with sustainable farming methods.

Working with nature

Supporters of sustainable development believe that it is very important to find **sustainable** ways of working alongside nature. In this way, people can allow the Earth to renew its **resources** through its natural processes.

Water management

Water management has been declared crucial by the **United Nations** and clean-up campaigns are being carried out in many polluted rivers and lakes. Water-saving projects are being created in both more and less developed countries. For example, in the Japanese city of Sumida, people have built rainfall collectors and installed special pedestrian walkways through which rainfall can flow and then sink back into the ground.

Tourism does not have to damage the environment. On this ecotour of a national park in Nepal, a small group of tourists is being carefully guided by local people.

Forest management

Managing forests well has become a very important issue, with many countries taking responsibility for protecting forest areas. But it is difficult to protect the forests whilst still providing work and income for people living in or near the area. Often, cutting down trees and selling the wood may be the only way that people can make a living in their local area. However, recent studies have shown that it can be much more profitable in the long run not to destroy a forest. A hectare of rainforest can be between 6 and 20 times more valuable if the products from it are harvested rather than being cut down for timber. In some parts of the rainforests, people are running projects that invest in harvesting rainforest products in a sustainable way. These products are then used for foods, medicine and cosmetics.

Sustainable tourism

In the past 50 years, the numbers of international tourists has exploded from 25 million to almost 1 billion. In the rush to attract tourists, large hotels and resorts have been built in less developed countries, destroying natural homes for plants and creatures and sometimes damaging historic or cultural sites. Many of these hotels are foreign-owned and import food from other countries. The result is that relatively little of the money, but all of the damage, stays in the less developed countries that the tourists visit.

Many people feel that tourism does not have to be run this way. They believe that in order to become sustainable, tourism needs to have less impact on the environment and involve local people far more. Supporters of sustainable tourism campaign against building giant resorts that damage the environment. They also urge holiday companies to buy more local produce and pay local people a fair wage.

Some countries are using the Internet, advertising campaigns and brochures to promote themselves to tourists so that the tourists can book directly, staying at local hotels and eating at local restaurants. Steps such as these may seem small, but if they were multiplied by the millions of tourists that visit less developed countries, they could have a major effect in helping to wipe out poverty.

Sustainable cities

More and more people are moving to large towns and cities, but this puts a great strain on these communities. In order to become **sustainable**, cities need to produce less pollution, generate less waste, use **resources** more efficiently and improve their inhabitants' quality of life. The American city of Seattle, for example, has created the Office of Sustainability and Environment (OSE), a department devoted to increasing sustainability in the city's services. The OSE has already helped reduce the use of chemical pesticides in the city's parks by 50 per cent. Seattle has also more than doubled the amount of solid waste it **recycles** and has cut water consumption per person by 20 per cent in the past fifteen years.

Cleaner transport

Transport issues are vital in making cities more sustainable. Most experts believe that it is essential to persuade people to give up their cars and use other, cleaner ways of travelling short distances in and around cities. In this way, people can reduce pollution and cut down on energy use. There have been some successes in introducing cleaner forms of transport, such as the electric trams in Manchester in the UK and Melbourne in Australia. Using electric trams helps to reduce the number of cars on the roads. Trams are also quiet and do not produce any polluting fumes.

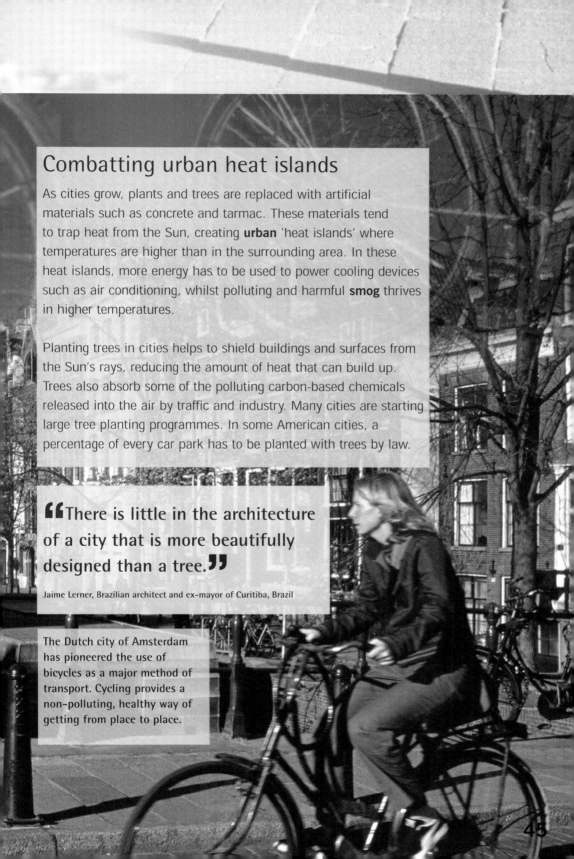

Combatting urban heat islands

As cities grow, plants and trees are replaced with artificial materials such as concrete and tarmac. These materials tend to trap heat from the Sun, creating **urban** 'heat islands' where temperatures are higher than in the surrounding area. In these heat islands, more energy has to be used to power cooling devices such as air conditioning, whilst polluting and harmful **smog** thrives in higher temperatures.

Planting trees in cities helps to shield buildings and surfaces from the Sun's rays, reducing the amount of heat that can build up. Trees also absorb some of the polluting carbon-based chemicals released into the air by traffic and industry. Many cities are starting large tree planting programmes. In some American cities, a percentage of every car park has to be planted with trees by law.

❝There is little in the architecture of a city that is more beautifully designed than a tree.❞

Jaime Lerner, Brazilian architect and ex-mayor of Curitiba, Brazil

The Dutch city of Amsterdam has pioneered the use of bicycles as a major method of transport. Cycling provides a non-polluting, healthy way of getting from place to place.

The case of Curitiba

How would life be if sustainable development could truly be achieved? Thirty-five years ago, the city of Curitiba in Brazil was facing typical problems, including a rapidly growing population, high pollution levels and poverty. But during the 1960s a group of young architects approached the city council with their suggestions for ways in which Curitiba could be developed. One of the architects, Jaime Lerner, became mayor on several occasions between 1971 and 1992, spending a total of twelve years in office. Today, Curitiba is home to 1.7 million people and is the closest thing to a **sustainable** city on the planet.

A better city

The people of Curitiba **recycle** around two thirds of their rubbish, more than the inhabitants of almost any other city. Poor families are able to bring their bags of sorted rubbish to centres where they can exchange them for bus tickets or food from nearby farms.

Education is a priority in the city, along with affordable housing. Workplaces, shops and homes all exist side by side in the same areas, which creates savings in travel expenses. A huge public transport system, which was designed to be cheap and reliable, carries almost two million passengers every day. Run-down buses are replaced by more efficient vehicles but the old buses are re-used, for example as adult education classrooms. The city centre is car-free and there are over 160 kilometres of cycle paths to encourage city dwellers away from motor vehicles. As a result, the city has a very low number of car-owners. It has slashed pollution and its citizens save an estimated 32 million litres of fuel per year.

Local involvement

Many of the changes in Curitiba rely on hundreds of small, cheap projects that call for local people to act as volunteers. For example, 1.5 million tree seedlings were provided by the city, but people in the local neighbourhoods were asked to plant and care for them. Many of these trees are found in the seventeen new parks created within the city, which also help to prevent flooding by diverting water into their lakes.

Curitiba still has problems, but surveys indicate that over 90 per cent of its people feel positive about living there. Part of this good feeling is created by the continuing involvement of local

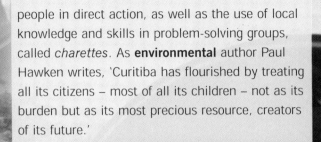

people in direct action, as well as the use of local knowledge and skills in problem-solving groups, called *charettes*. As **environmental** author Paul Hawken writes, 'Curitiba has flourished by treating all its citizens – most of all its children – not as its burden but as its most precious resource, creators of its future.'

Around 70 per cent of Curitiba's commuters use the city's energy-efficient public transport system to travel to and from work.

❝The dream of a better city is always in the heads of its residents. If people feel respected, they will assume responsibility to help solve other problems.❞

Jaime Lerner, architect and ex-mayor of Curitiba

What can you do?

This book shows the reasons for introducing sustainable development and the problems faced by its supporters. It also shows a few of the ways in which ideas and actions that promote sustainable development are being carried out all over the world.

Every effort helps

No one person can save the Earth by themselves, but that doesn't mean that individuals are powerless. Everyone can make a contribution to living in a more **sustainable** way. Together, these individual contributions can grow into major worldwide change.

Some projects and programmes are large and expensive or require governments or big businesses to organize and run them. Many others are simple, cost very little and only need the effort of small numbers of local people. Both levels of action are essential if sustainable development is to be achieved.

Most **environmental** schemes set up by national and local governments are voluntary. They require individuals to join in to make them successful. For example, the US EnergyStar programme promotes energy-efficient products, but **consumers** must actually buy EnergyStar labelled goods for the scheme to work. Thinking about what you buy and how you use and discard items is one important way that individuals can help. Gaining more information and talking to other people is another.

You can make a difference

Here is a list of some of the ways in which you can make a difference. Most of the suggestions come from the **United Nations** Sustainable Development Information Pack.

These schoolchildren are taking part in a project to clean up a river. Small-scale, local projects like this can make a real difference to the environment.

48

Save energy and resources

- Turn off appliances, such as TVs, light bulbs and computers, when they are not being used.
- Use low-energy lights and appliances.
- Use less water, for example by taking quick showers instead of baths, and turning off the tap while brushing your teeth.

Travel sensibly

- Where possible, walk, cycle and use public transport.
- Make fewer car journeys and share lifts with others.

Shop sensibly

- Avoid products with wasteful packaging.
- Choose environmentally friendly products.

Reduce waste

- Re-use old bags, bottles and containers.
- Don't throw things away when they can be fixed.
- Find your local **recycling** centre and make use of it.

Help nature

- Avoid using garden chemicals and look for 'natural' alternatives.
- Plant native trees, flowers and shrubs (rather than plants from foreign places).

Become involved

- Search your local library notice boards and newspapers for local **conservation** projects.
- Ask a teacher about setting up a school sustainability project.
- Join in with 'cleaning and greening' projects to remove pollution from your local environment.

Facts and figures

How much rubbish?

This table shows the amounts of rubbish (including paper, cardboard, cans, bottles and other solid products) created by the people of different countries in one year.

United States	190,204,000 tonnes
Japan	50,536,000 tonnes
Russia	50,000,000 tonnes
Germany	36,976,000 tonnes
Mexico	29,272,000 tonnes
France	28,800,000 tonnes
United Kingdom	28,000,000 tonnes
Italy	26,605,000 tonnes
Turkey	20,253,000 tonnes
South Korea	18,223,000 tonnes

Source: The Economist Pocket World In Figures, 2002

Paper recycling

This table shows the percentage of paper recovered for **recycling** in different countries.

Germany	70%
Austria	69%
New Zealand	66%
Switzerland	63%
Netherlands	62%
Sweden	62%
Finland	57%
South Korea	57%
Japan	54%
Australia	50%
United States	41%
United Kingdom	40%

Source: The Economist Pocket World In Figures, 2002

Deforestation

This table shows the approximate area of forests destroyed between 1990 and 2000.

Brazil	22,264 sq km
Indonesia	13,124 sq km
Sudan	9,589 sq km
Zambia	8,509 sq km
Mexico	6,306 sq km
Congo	5,324 sq km
Myanmar	5,169 sq km
Nigeria	3,984 sq km
Zimbabwe	3,199 sq km
Argentina	2,851 sq km

Source: The Economist Pocket World In Figures, 2002

Health and education

In Italy, there is one doctor for every 169 people. In Chad, Eritrea, the Gambia and Malawi, there is one doctor for every 50,000 people.

Access to essential medical drugs is limited in many poorer countries. In over 20 ˙ countries less than half the population have access to essential drugs. In Nigeria, the figure is just 10%.

In Japan, the average life expectancy is 81.5 years, in the United Kingdom, it is 78.2 and in the United States, 77.5. In Zimbabwe, the average life expectancy is 42.9 years whilst in Burundi it is just 36.1.

Less than half the adults of 25 countries of the world can read and write. Only 14.3% of the adults in the African country of Niger are able to read and write.

Environmental Sustainability Index 2002

Developed by the World Economic Forum, and Yale and Columbia universities, the Environmental Sustainability Index is designed as a measure of a country's progress towards a **sustainable** environment. Sixty-eight different indicators were measured, including air quality in cities, water management and the strength of the country's laws on the environment.

Top 25 (scored out of 100):

1	Finland	73.9
2	Norway	73.0
3	Sweden	72.6
4	Canada	70.6
5	Switzerland	66.5
6	Uruguay	66.0
7	Austria	64.2
8	Iceland	63.9
9	Costa Rica	63.2
10	Latvia	63.0
11	Hungary	62.7
12	Croatia	62.5
13	Botswana	61.8
14	Slovakia	61.6
15	Argentina	61.5
16	Australia	60.3
17	Panama	60.0
18	Estonia	60.0
19	New Zealand	59.9
20	Brazil	59.6
21	Bolivia	59.4
22	Colombia	59.1
23	Slovenia	58.8
24	Albania	57.9
25	Paraguay	57.8

Bottom 25:

118	Uzbekistan	41.3
119	Rwanda	40.6
120	Oman	40.2
121	Trinidad and Tobago	40.1
122	Jamaica	40.1
123	Niger	39.4
124	Libya	39.3
125	Belgium	39.1
126	Mauritania	38.9
127	Guinea-Bissau	38.8
128	Madagascar	38.8
129	China	38.5
130	Liberia	37.7
131	Turkmenistan	37.3
132	Somalia	37.1
133	Nigeria	36.7
134	Sierra Leone	36.5
135	South Korea	35.9
136	Ukraine	35.0
137	Haiti	34.8
138	Saudi Arabia	34.2
139	Iraq	33.2
140	North Korea	32.3
141	United Arab Emirates	25.7
142	Kuwait	23.9

Source: Columbia University Center for International Earth Science Information Network (CIESIN).

Further information

International contacts

The Earth Council
PO Box 319-6100
San Jose
Costa Rica
email: eci@ecouncil.ac.cr
www.ecouncil.ac.cr

International Institute for Sustainable Development
161 Portage Avenue East, 6th Floor
Winnipeg
Manitoba
R3B 0Y4
Canada
email: info@iisd.ca
www.iisd.org

World Business Council for Sustainable Development
4 Chemin de Conches
1231 Conches-Geneva
Switzerland
Tel: (41) 22 839 3100
email: info@wbcsd.org
www.wbcsd.ch

Contacts in the UK

Centre For Alternative Technology
Machynlleth
Powys SYO 9AZ
Wales
Tel: 01654 702400
email: info@catinfo.demon.co.uk
www.cat.org.uk

Friends of the Earth
26-28 Underwood Street
London N1 7JQ
Tel: 020 7490 1555
email: info@uk.greenpeace.org
www.foe.co.uk

Sustainable Development Commission
A505, Romney House
Tufton Street
London SW1P 3RA
Tel: 020 7944 4964
email: sd.commission@defra.gsi.gov.uk
www.sd-commission.gov.uk

Sustainable Development International
Henley Publishing Ltd
Trans-World House
100 City Road
London EC1Y 2BP
Tel: 020 7871 0123
www.sustdev.org/contact

United Nations Association Sustainable Development Unit
3 Whitehall Court
London SW1A 2EL
Tel: 020 7839 1784

Contacts in the USA

Division for Sustainable Development
United Nations Department of Economic and Social Affairs
Two United Nations Plaza
DC2-2220
New York, NY 10017
email: dsd@un.org
www.un.org/esa/sustdev

The Foundation for Global Sustainability
PO Box 1101
Knoxville, TN 37901-1101
www.korrnet.org/fgs

Friends of the Earth
1025 Vermont Avenue NW,
Washington, DC 20005-6303
www.foe.org

National Center for Appropriate Technology
3040 Continental Drive
PO Box 3838
Butte, MT 59701
www.ncat.org

Sierra Club
85 Second Street
San Francisco
CA 94105-3441
www.sierraclub.org

Contacts in Australia

Energy Resource of Australia
1 Macquarie Place
Sydney
NSW 2000
Tel: (61) 2 9256 8900

Friends of the Earth
PO Box 2222
Fitzroy
Victoria 3065
Tel: (61) 3 9419 8700
email: foe@foe.org.au
www.foe.org.au

United Nations Information Centre Australia
125 York Street
Sydney
NSW 2000
Tel: (61) 2 9238 1144
www.un.org.au/aboutus.htm

The Internet

Centre for Global Development
www.cgdev.org/wrn/factsinfigures.html

Centre for Renewable Energy and Sustainable Technology
www.crest.org

Envirolink Online Library
www.envirolink.org

Sustainable Earth Exchange
www.class.csupomona.edu/earth.html

US Department of Energy
Smart Communities pages
www.sustainable.doe.gov

A massive collection of links to sustainable development websites
www.ecosustainable.com.au/links.htm

Glossary

acid rain
rain or snow that contains poisonous or harmful chemicals created by burning fossil fuels

Agenda 21
plan of action made at the Earth Summit in 1992 to promote sustainable development

atmosphere
collection of different gases that surround the Earth

biodiversity
range of different species within an area. Biodiversity is short for biological diversity. The more biodiverse an area is, the more species it contains.

boycott
to refuse to take part in something or buy something, as a way of making a protest

Brundtland Commission
important commission, whose full name is the World Commission on Environment and Development (WCED), which was held in 1987 and produced a report on sustainable development

CFCs
CFCs is short for chlorofluorocarbons, chemicals developed in the early 20th century and used in industry, in refrigerators and aerosol cans. They have since been found to be damaging to part of the atmosphere.

conservation
protection of the environment and natural resources of the Earth, including its plant and animal life

consumer
someone who buys and uses goods and services

deforestation
cutting down of large numbers of trees for fuel or timber, or to clear the land for settlements or farming

development
ways in which the human population improve their standard of living and their quality of life

economic
to do with the way money is made and used. Economic development is the increase in a country's ability to produce goods and services in order to create more money, usually though larger and more efficient industries.

enhanced greenhouse effect
build-up of carbon dioxide, methane and other gases in the atmosphere, trapping the Sun's heat and affecting the climate

environmental
to do with the natural world of the land, sea and air

extinction
permanent disappearance of a species

global warming
warming of the Earth's atmosphere, believed to be due to the increase in the greenhouse gases in the atmosphere

greenhouse gases
gases, such as carbon dioxide, methane, water vapour and nitrous oxide, in the atmosphere that trap heat from the Sun and warm the Earth

habitat
surroundings that a particular species needs to survive. Some creatures can live in more than one habitat.

Industrial Revolution
change in the way goods were produced that started in the UK over 200 years ago and involved the building of large factories and machinery

initiative
new plan or a new way of acting

non-renewable resources
resources that cannot be replaced once they have been used. Oil and coal are examples of non-renewable resources.

nutrient
any material taken in by a living thing to help it keep alive

ozone layer
layer of ozone gas in the Earth's atmosphere that absorbs a large amount of harmful rays from the Sun

raw materials
resources such as oil, wood or stone that are used to make other materials or products

recycling
recovery or re-use of waste materials to make new products

renewable resources
resources such as water or the wind that are not used up over time

resources
natural things found on Earth such as water, rocks, wood and coal that can be used in some way

smog
mixture of fog and smoke that sometimes hangs in the air over cities and industrial areas

social
to do with the way people live together. Social development involves changes and improvements to aspects of human society such as education and healthcare.

soil erosion
process by which loose soil is washed or blown away

solar panel
device that takes energy from the Sun and converts it into electricity

solar power
power from the Sun that can be used for heating, lighting etc.

Soviet Union
large communist country that was formed from Russia and neighbouring countries in 1922 and lasted until 1991

species
group of animals or plants that share the same characteristics

summit
important meeting between leaders of countries, organizations or businesses

sustainable
able to be continued without causing damage

technology
use of science to do practical things

United Nations (UN)
international organization that was set up in 1945 to encourage world peace

urban
to do with towns or cities

wind turbine
device rather like a windmill that converts the energy in wind into electricity

Index